# Workbook

# BACKPACK Gold

## 2

**Mario Herrera • Diane Pinkley**

Pearson Education
Edinburgh Gate, Harlow
Essex, CM20 2JE
England
and Associated Companies throughout the World

www.pearsonelt.com

Authorised adaptation from the United States edition entitled Backpack,
second edition, by Mario Herrera and Diane Pinkley. Published by Pearson
Education, Inc. Copyright © 2009 Pearson Education, Inc.

Backpack Gold published by Pearson Education Ltd. Copyright © 2010 Pearson
Education Ltd.

Ninth impression 2016

ISBN: 978 1 4082 4504 0

Set in 16pt HSP Helvetica

Printed in Malaysia (CTP-VVP)

Illustrations: Aubrey, Meg, 55, 56; Berlin, Rose Mary, 26, 65, 78; Bowser, Ken,
9, 12, 14, 34, 36; Boyer, Robin, 72; Bridy, Dan, 4, 16, 24, 33, 36;  Briseno, Luis,
11, 18, 30, 44, 66, 73; Burrows, Phill, 87, 104; Catanese, Donna, 8, 38, 41, 58,
82, 84;  Cleyet-Merle, Laurence, 7; Davis, Billy, 2; Dillard, Sarah, 28, 86; Dowty,
Bridget, 12, 13, 14, 18, 82, 83, 84, 87; Durrel, Julie, 1, 3; Flanagan, Kate, 6, 18,
34, 43, 46, 54, 81; Klug, Dave, 34, 52, 53; Miranda, Hugo, 7, 31, 61, 91–108;
Newman, Fran, 23, 53; Pye, Trevor, 31, 32, 61, 62, 63, 64, 78; Sexton, Brenda,
71; Smith, Jaime, 42, 44, 48; Stormer, Brooks, Karen. 87

Photo Credits: l = left, c = centre, r = right, t = top, b = bottom
The publisher would like to thank the following for their kind permission to
reproduce their photographs:

iStockphoto: 22c, 37br, 73, 81, 96; Jupiter Unlimited: 37bl, 74 (2), 74 (3), 74
(1); PhotoDisc: 43; Photolibrary.com: Fancy 22t; shutterstock: 37cr; Travel Stock
Photography: photographersdirect.com 37cl

All other images © Pearson Education, Inc

Every effort has been made to trace the copyright holders and we apologise
in advance for any unintentional omissions. We would be pleased to insert the
appropriate acknowledgement in any subsequent edition of this publication.

# Contents

# **1** First Day of Class

**Listen. Draw lines to match.
Colour the pictures to match.**

## Time for School!

I've got a | blue pencil. |

I've got a | red pen. |

I've got a | green backpack. |

School time again!

I've got | pink rubbers. |

I've got glue and tape.

I've got a | white ruler. |

School time is great!

I've got | purple notebooks. |

My markers are cool.

They go in my backpack.

Let's walk to school.

**2** **Match. Write. Use words from the box.**

| 11 eleven | 12 twelve | 14 fourteen |
|-----------|-----------|-------------|
| 16 sixteen | 18 eighteen | 20 twenty |

1. There are _____*twelve*_____ stickers.

2. There are _____ markers.

3. There are _____ crayons.

4. There are _____ pencils.

5. There are _____ pens.

6. There are _____ rubbers.

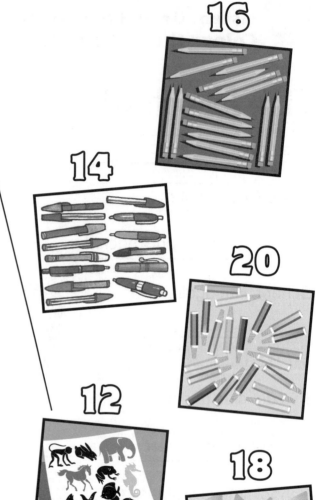

## Grammar

| She's<br>He's<br>They're | walking to the door. | she's = she is<br>he's = he is<br>they're = they are |
|---|---|---|

 **Look. Write *She's, He's* or *They're*.**

1. _____ glueing shapes.

2. _____ listening to a story.

3. _____ cutting paper.

 **Look. Write. Use words from the box.**

| singing   talking   walking |

1. They're _____.  2. He's _____.  3. She's _____.

**5** **Look. Write.**

1. What is he doing?

   _He's reading._

2. What is she doing?

   _____

3. What are they doing?

   _____

**Grammar**

**There is** one computer.
**There are** five desks.

**6** **Write *There is* or *There are*. Draw.**

_____ one ball.         _____ seven crayons.

4

**Find the words and circle them.**

| x | p | y | m | e | z | r | s | o | c | d |
|---|---|---|---|---|---|---|---|---|---|---|
| u | c | o | u | n | t | i | n | g | s | p |
| l | o | y | b | h | u | z | q | v | u | r |
| z | l | c | g | o | x | y | r | h | h | t |
| x | o | p | e | n | i | n | g | q | k | a |
| i | u | i | d | l | n | z | m | w | g | l |
| l | r | p | n | d | u | o | z | y | h | k |
| s | i | t | t | i | n | g | v | f | l | i |
| w | n | z | j | u | q | o | r | l | x | n |
| u | g | j | x | r | e | a | d | i | n | g |

colouring
counting
opening
reading
sitting
talking

 **Read and write. Draw and colour.**

Two friends are in the playground. What are they doing?

They're _____.

**9** **Listen and write.**

1. _____ crayons.

2. _____ notebooks.

3. She's _____.

4. He's _____.

5. They're _____.

**10** **Listen. Write. Match.**

# School Is Cool!

I am cutting, I am glueing,

    I am _____, too.

I like school. School is cool!

He is reading, he is writing,

    he is _____, too.

He likes school. School is cool!

She is talking, she is playing,

    she is _____, too.

She likes school. School is cool!

# The Special Backpack

**11** **Read _The Special Backpack_. Write _yes_ or _no_.**

1. There are sixteen purple paper clips. _____yes_____

2. There are three yellow pencils. _____

3. There are five white rulers. _____

4. There are fourteen pink rubbers. _____

5. There are nine green pens. _____

6. There are twelve stickers. _____

7. There are eleven red markers. _____

8. There is one special backpack. _____

**12** **What is in _your_ backpack? Write how many.**

_There is one apple in my backpack._

_____

_____

_____

_____

_____

_____

**Work with a partner. Say what's in your backpack.**

# Review

**13** **Look and read. Circle a sentence.**

1. She's cutting paper.

   (She's colouring pictures.)

2. They're talking.

   They're counting.

3. He's writing a story.

   He's listening to a story.

**14** **Look. Write a sentence.**

1. _She's rubbing out._ _____

2. _____

3. _____

**15** **What are you doing? Write a sentence.**

_____

_____

# Cut-out Activity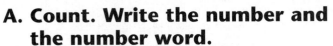

**A. Count. Write the number and the number word.**

**B. Cut out the cards. Find a partner. Talk about How many.**

How many boxes are there?

There are eleven boxes.

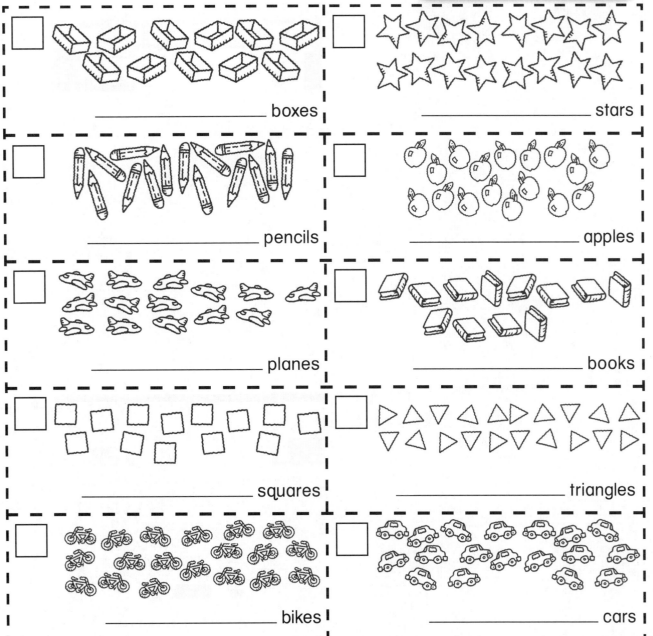

_____ boxes

_____ stars

_____ pencils

_____ apples

_____ planes

_____ books

_____ squares

_____ triangles

_____ bikes

_____ cars

# Fun and Games

**1** **Listen and write. Draw lines to match.**

## Hide and Seek

*I close my eyes and my friends run!*
*Ready or not, here I come.*

Where is Lucy? Now I see!

She's _____ the swing, next to Dee.

behind

Where is Peter? Now I see!

He's high up there _____ the tree.

*I close my eyes and my friends run!*
*Ready or not, here I come.*

Where is Alice? Now I see!

She's _____ the bush, in front of me.

under

Where are you? Now I see!
You're right here, looking at me.

*I close my eyes and my friends run!*
*Ready or not, here I come.*

in

**2** **Look. Write. Use words from the box.**

| behind | between | in | in front of | on | under |
|---|---|---|---|---|---|

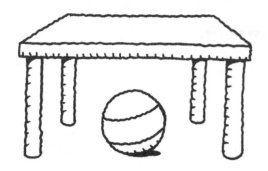

1. The ball is _____ the table.

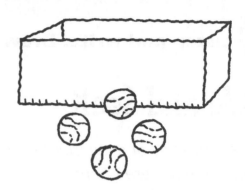

2. The marbles are _____ the box.

3. The frog is _____ the tree and the bush.

4. The kite is _____ the tree.

5. The backpack is _____ the chair.

6. The cat is _____ the backpack.

## Grammar

| He / She | **likes** catching and throwing. |
| I / They | **like** catching and throwing. |

**3** **Write *like* or *likes*.**

1. They _____ playing chess.

2. He _____ flying kites.

3. She _____ climbing trees.

4. They _____ playing hide and seek.

5. I _____ skipping.

6. She _____ skating.

**4** **Look. Draw lines to match. Write the answers.**

1. What does she like doing?

   _____

playing chess

2. What does he like doing?

   _____

skipping

3. What do they like doing?

   _____

riding a bike

Unit 2

13

## 5 Count and write the number word.

| 10 ten | 20 twenty | 30 thirty | 40 forty | 50 fifty | 60 sixty |

_____ten_____ chess pieces

_____ dominoes

_____ marbles

_____ cards

## 6 Write the number word. Draw.

There are 10 chess pieces.

There are _____ chess pieces.

There are 20 marbles.

There are _____ marbles.

**7** **Write. Use words from the box.**

ball
bike
chess
kite
trees

1. I like flying a _____.

2. I like catching and throwing a _____.

3. I like playing _____ with my friends.

4. I like climbing _____ in the park.

5. I like riding a _____.

**8** **What do you like doing? Draw and colour. Write.**

I like _____.

Unit 2

15

**9 Listen and write.**

1. His football is _____ his bed.

2. Her notebook is _____ her backpack.

3. Their bikes are _____ the tree.

**10 Listen. Draw lines to match.**

# Having Fun

I like flying my kite in the sky.
I'm not the only one.
My friends like flying kites in the sky.
We are having fun!

I like riding my bike in the park.
I'm not the only one.
My friends like riding bikes in the park.
We are having fun!

I like throwing a ball in the air.
I'm not the only one.
My friends like throwing balls in the air.
We are having fun!

**11 Write your own verse. Draw a picture.**

I like _____ my _____

    in the _____.

I'm not the only one.

My friends like _____

    in the _____.

We are having fun!

16

# Playing Games

What do they like doing?

They like throwing balls.

**12** **Read *Playing Games*. Write. Tick (✔) the boxes.**

 1

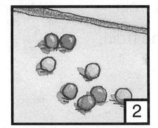 2

 3

 4

| What do they like doing? | balls | cards | chalk | marbles |
|---|---|---|---|---|
| 1. Children from Argentina like throwing ___balls___. | ✔ | | | |
| 2. Children from Indonesia like rolling _____. | | | | |
| 3. Children from England like playing a game with _____. | | | | |
| 4. Children from Spain like turning over _____. | | | | |

**13** **Where are you from? What do children from your country like to play? Write.**

I am from _____.

Children from _____ like playing _____.

# Review

  **Count and write.**

1. There are ____20____ counters in front of the table.

2. There are _____ counters on the table.

3. There are _____ counters next to the snake.

4. There are _____ counters between the snake and the giraffe.

5. There are _____ circles on the train.

6. There are _____ squares on the train.

  **Write the word.**
**Draw lines to match.**

1. They like ___playing___ chess.

2. She likes _____ her bike.

3. He likes _____ trees.

4. They like _____ kites.

5. She likes _____ marbles.

| riding |

| playing |

| flying |

| rolling |

| climbing |

# Cut-out Activity ✂ - - - - - - - - - - -

**A. Draw pictures.**
   **Cut out the cards.**
**B. Find a partner.**
   **Talk about where things are.**

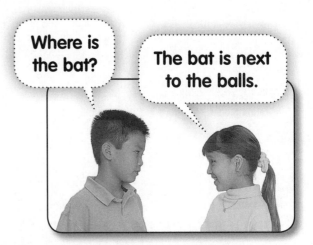

Where is the bat?

The bat is next to the balls.

| behind | between | in front of | next to | on |
|---|---|---|---|---|

| a backpack | a bat | a cat | a skipping rope |
|---|---|---|---|
| a kite | three worms | two balls | two birds |

# Our New House

**1** **Listen and write. Use words from the box.**

| Aunt | brother | cousins | family | father |
| grandfather | grandmother | mother | Uncle | |

## My Family

*Don't be shy – come and talk to me.*

*Meet the people in my _____!*

Here's my _____, my sister

and _____.

That little baby is my new _____!

Say hello to my _____ Lou,

_____ Sally and my

_____, too!

Over there is my _____ Jill.

That tall man is my _____ Bill.

*Don't be shy – come and talk to me.*

*Meet the people in my family!*

## Write. Use words from the box. Draw.

| aunt | cousins | grandfather | grandmother | uncle |

1. These are my aunt's children.

   They are my _____.

2. This is my mother's mother.

   She is my _____.

3. This is my mother's sister.

   She is my _____.

4. This is my mother's brother.

   He is my _____.

5. This is my mother's father.

   He is my _____.

6. And this is ME!

| | | |
|---|---|---|
| **Where's** your mother? | **She's** in the living room. | where's = where is |
| | | he's/she's = he is/she is |
| **Where's** the sink? | **It's** in the kitchen. | it's = it is |
| **Where are** your cousins? | **They're** in the kitchen. | they're = they are |

 **Look. Write.**

1. Where's your brother?

_____ in the dining room.

2. Where are your mother and father?

_____ in the living room.

3. Where's Aunt Ella?

_____ in the bedroom.

4. Where's the fridge?

_____ in the kitchen.

 **Where's your mirror? Write.**

_____

_____

 **Write *Where's* or *Where are*.**

1. _____ the lamp?

2. _____ the plants?

3. _____ the curtains?

4. _____ the mirror?

5. _____ the shelves?

**6** **Find and colour. Ask a friend where these things are in a house.**

chair    lamp   rug
cooker   bath   television

**Find the words and circle them.**

| m | t | k | i | t | c | h | e | n | w | s |
|---|---|---|---|---|---|---|---|---|---|---|
| y | b | a | t | c | e | o | m | m | i | r |
| v | a | c | h | l | u | t | i | p | k | h |
| e | t | w | t | u | g | r | m | k | s | t |
| c | h | a | i | r | a | d | i | j | t | w |
| o | r | p | a | b | e | d | r | o | o | m |
| y | o | t | w | t | u | g | r | u | o | g |
| o | o | n | a | d | h | j | o | k | t | u |
| e | m | w | t | u | g | r | r | o | s | t |

bathroom
bedroom
chair
kitchen
mirror

 **What's your favourite room? What's in it?
Write. Draw and colour.**

I like my _____.

In this room, there's a _____ and a _____.

**9** **Listen and circle.**

1. Anna's desk is **behind** / **under** the window.

2. Her **computer** / **notebook** is on her desk.

3. There's a **chair** / **bedside table** next to her bed.

4. Her bedside table has a **clock** / **radio** on it.

5. Her bedroom is mostly **blue and green** / **pink and white**.

**10** **Listen and write. Colour to match.**

# What Colour Is Your Bedroom?

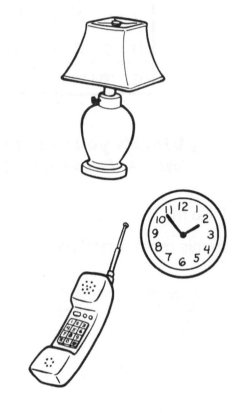

Joe's bedroom is all in _____ –
   his rug and his mirror,
   and his clock and bed!

Sue's bedroom is all in _____ –
   her wardrobe and her phone,
   and her answering machine!

My bedroom is all in _____ –
   my lamp and my curtains,
   my computer, too!

**11** **What colours are in your bedroom? Write.**

> I have a blue desk and a white chair.

_____

_____

_____

_____

26

# Moving Day

**12**  **Read** *Moving Day.* **Circle** *yes* **or** *no.*

| Rooms in Sonia's New House | | |
|---|---|---|
| computer room | yes | no |
| dining room | yes | no |
| kitchen | yes | no |
| living room | yes | no |
| playroom | yes | no |
| three bedrooms | yes | no |

| Things in Sonia's New Bedroom | | |
|---|---|---|
| bed | yes | no |
| chair | yes | no |
| lamp | yes | no |
| rug | yes | no |
| table | yes | no |
| television | yes | no |

**13**  **What do you have in your bedroom? Circle** *yes* **or** *no.* **Write a sentence.**

_____

_____

_____

| bed | yes | no |
|---|---|---|
| chair | yes | no |
| lamp | yes | no |
| rug | yes | no |
| table | yes | no |
| television | yes | no |

# Review

 **Read, look and draw.**

1. Draw a clock in the kitchen.
2. Draw a lamp in the bedroom.
3. Draw curtains at the bedroom window.
4. Draw a plant on the dining room table.
5. Draw a rug in the dining room.

 **Choose the best word. Tick.**

1. The fridge is in the _____.    ☐ living room    ☑ kitchen
2. The bath is in the _____.    ☐ kitchen    ☐ bathroom
3. The bedside table is in the _____.    ☐ dining room    ☐ bedroom
4. The sink is in the _____.    ☐ kitchen    ☐ living room

# Cut-out Activity ✂ - - - - - - - - - - - - - - -

**A. Where is it in a house? Cut and glue.**
**B. Work with a partner.**

Where are the beds?

They're in the bedroom.

bedroom

bathroom

living room

kitchen

dining room

| beds | cupboards | chairs | clock | wardrobe | lamp |
| mirror | picture | fridge | rug | shelves | shower |
| sink | sofa | cooker | table | bath | television |

## C. Draw and colour.

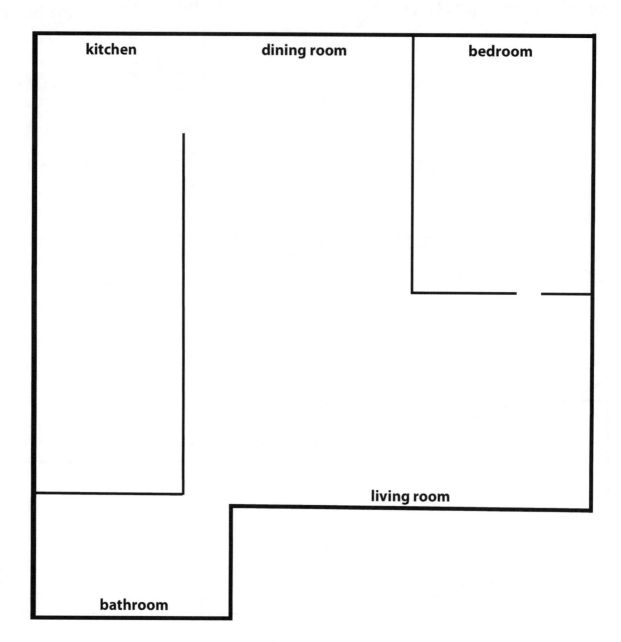

# 4 My Town

**1 Listen and write. Circle the picture.**

## Shopping in Town

I love going to town.
There's so much to see.

Daddy, there's a _____.

Let's get some _____ for me!

I love going to town.
There's so much to see.
Please, please, please,
      Daddy, please!

I love going to town.
There's so much to see.

Mummy, there's a _____.

Let's get a _____ for me!

I love going to town.
There's so much to see.
Please, please, please,
      Mummy, please!

Please, Daddy, please!
Mummy, please!

**2** **Look. Write. Use words from the box.**

## Our Neighbourhood

| between | in | next to | on the corner |
|---------|-----|---------|---------------|

1. The greengrocer's shop is _____ the bookshop and the video shop.

2. The toy shop is _____ the cinema.

3. The restaurant is _____ the fire station.

4. There is a computer shop _____.

5. There is a shoe shop _____ our neighbourhood.

6. There is a video shop _____.

Is there a restaurant on Back Street?

Are there two video shops on Park Street?

Yes, there is.
No, there isn't.
Yes, there are.
No, there aren't.

**3** **Look. Write** *Yes, there is* **or** *No, there isn't.*

1. Is there a police station on Spring Street? _____

2. Is there a video shop next to the police station? _____

3. Is there a bus station on the corner? _____

**4** **Look. Write** *Yes, there are* **or** *No, there aren't.*

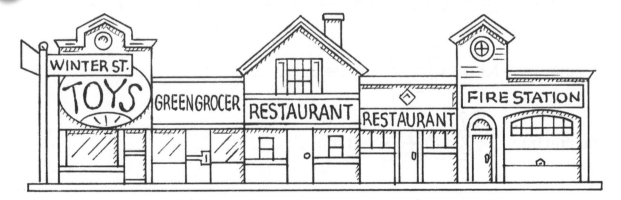

1. Are there any bookshops on Winter Street? _____

2. Are there two toy shops on Winter Street? _____

3. Are there two restaurants between the greengrocer's shop and the fire

station? _____

**5** **Write *Is there* or *Are there*. Look. Ask and answer.**

1. _____ any restaurants on Back Street?

2. _____ a supermarket on Main Street?

3. _____ any banks on Main Street?

4. _____ a toy shop on Back Street?

5. _____ a music shop on Main Street?

**6** **Look. Write. Use words from the box.**

| computer shop | fire station | restaurant | shoe shop | toy shop |

1. You can buy  at the _____.

2. You can shop for a  at the _____.

3. You can buy  at the _____.

4. You can see a  at the _____.

5. You can eat  at the _____.

**What is it? Read. Write the missing letters. Answer the question.**

1. You can buy a bus ticket here.
2. You can buy shoes here.
3. You can post a letter here.
4. You can get money here.

5. You can buy music here.
6. You can buy toys here.
7. You can buy videos here.
8. You can try out computers here.

9.

1. b u s   s t a t i o n
2. _ _ _ e _ _ _ _
3. _ o _ _ _ _ _ _ _ _
4. _ a _ _ _
5. _ u _ _ _ _ _ _ _
6. _ _ _ _ _ _ p _
7. v _ _ _ _ _ _ _ _
8. _ _ _ _ _ _ _ _ _ _

9. Where can you buy books? _____

 **Choose two places. Draw and colour. Write the names.**

bank

fire station

music shop

restaurant

shoe shop

supermarket

toy shop

video shop

**9** **Listen. Tick *yes* or *no*.**

yes   no

1. There's a bank on the corner of Pine Street and River Road.  ☐ ☐

2. The shoe shop is on Martin Street, next to the bus station.  ☐ ☐

3. The post office is on Hill Street, near the hospital.  ☐ ☐

4. The restaurant is on Park Road, between the computer shop and the music shop.  ☐ ☐

5. Michael's new house is the one with the blue door, on the corner.  ☐ ☐

6. There's a toy shop on the corner of Oak Street and Bennett Street.  ☐ ☐

**10** **Listen and circle. Connect the letters.**

# My City Kitty

My curious kitty likes the city.
She plays in town all day.
Is she here in the **music / computer** shop?
(Meow, meow) Here kitty, kitty!

My curious kitty likes the city.
She plays in town all day.
Is she here in the **grocer's / video** shop?
(Meow, meow) Here kitty, kitty!

My curious kitty likes the city.
She plays in town all day.
Is she here in the **bank / restaurant**?
(Meow, meow) Here kitty, kitty!

# Places Around the World

**What is it?**

**Where is it?**

**It's a castle.**

**In Japan.**

---

**11** **Read *Places Around the World*. Draw lines to match *where* it is to *what* it is.**

1. 
   Kenya
   in Africa

2. 
   London
   in England

3. 
   Japan
   in Asia

4. 
   Paris
   in France

---

**12** **What amazing place is in your town, city or country? Write.**

_____

_____

# Review

 **Look. Tick** *next to*, *between* **or** *on the corner*. **Write.**

1. The fire station is _____ the shoe shop.

   ☐ next to          ☐ between          ☐ on the corner

2. The bank is _____.

   ☐ next to          ☐ between          ☐ on the corner

3. The shoe shop is _____ the bank and the fire station.

   ☐ next to          ☐ between          ☐ on the corner

---

**Look at activity 13. Write** *Yes, there is* **or** *No, there isn't.*

1. Is there a police station next to the cinema?

   _____

2. Is there a supermarket between the police station and the cinema?

   _____

3. Is there a fire station on the corner?

   _____

---

**Answer the questions.**

1. Where can you get money? _____

2. Where can you buy food? _____

# Cut-out Activity ✂-----------------

**A. Work with a partner.**
**Cut and glue.**
**B. Ask questions and copy.**

Is there a computer shop on Water Street?

Yes, there is. It's on the corner, next to the cinema.

| | computer shop | | supermarket |
|---|---|---|---|
| | cinema | **Water Street** | fire station |
| | | | |
| | | | post office |
| **bank** | | | |

**Green Street** — — — — — — — — —

| train station | | | hospital |
|---|---|---|---|

| | | | |
|---|---|---|---|
| bookshop | bus station | police station | restaurant |
| school | shoe shop | toy shop | video shop |

# 5 My Busy Family

**1  Listen and write. Draw lines to match.**

## Working Hard!

*Monday, Tuesday, Wednesday,*
*    Thursday, Friday, too.*
*We work hard all week long.*
*We're busy, busy, busy!*

My _____'s a chef in
   a restaurant.
He's busy!

My _____'s a nurse in
   a hospital.
She's busy!

My _____ makes toy robots.
He's busy!

My _____ studies hard at school.
She's busy!

Monday, Tuesday, Wednesday,
    Thursday, Friday, too.
We work hard all week long.
We're busy, busy, busy!

**2** **Write. Use words from the box.**

| | | |
|---|---|---|
| factory | hospital | lab |
| restaurant | school | shop |

1. A factory worker works in a _____.

2. A teacher works in a _____.

3. A chef works in a _____.

4. A nurse works in a _____.

5. A shopkeeper works in a _____.

6. A scientist works in a _____.

## Grammar

| am | I **am** a teacher. | |
|----|-----|-----|
| are | You **are** a student. | They **are** students. |
| is | He **is** a student. | She **is** a student. |

 **Write _am_, _is_ or _are_.**

1. She _____ a dancer.

2. I _____ a musician.

3. They _____ actors.

4. She _____ a firefighter.

5. You _____ a student.

6. He _____ a pilot.

## Grammar

| I | I **work** in a shop. | |
|----|-----|-----|
| he/she | He **works** in a shop. | She **works** in a shop. |
| you/they | You **work** in a shop. | They **work** in a shop. |

 **Write _work_ or _works_.**

1. They _____ in a lab.

2. I _____ in a hospital.

3. He _____ in a factory.

4. You _____ in a school.

5. She _____ in a restaurant.

6. I _____ in a theatre.

**5** **Write. Use words from the box.**

1. A nurse _____.

2. A footballer _____.

3. A pilot _____.

4. An actor _____.

5. A chef _____.

cooks food

flies planes

works in a hospital

makes films

plays football

**6** **Look. Write.**

1. What does she do?

   _She makes music._

2. What does he do?

   _____

3. What does he do?

   _____

4. What does he do?

   _____

44

**7** **Do the crossword puzzle. Write the words.**

**Across** →

1. He works in a shop.
2. She flies planes.
3. He works in a hospital.
4. She works in a restaurant.

**Down** ↓

5. She makes music.
6. He makes films.
7. She does experiments.
8. He puts out fires.

1. s h o p k e e p e r

**8** **What does your family do? Draw and colour. Write.**

My _____ is a _____. He _____.

My _____ is a _____. She _____.

**9** **Listen and circle.**

1. Mrs Smith is a **doctor / dancer**.

2. Carol's uncle is an **actor / artist**.

3. Mark's father is a **teacher / scientist**.

4. Mr Martin is a **chef / footballer**.

5. Linda's mum is a **factory worker / housewife**.

6. Iris wants to be a **photographer / musician**.

TRACK 17

**10** **Listen and write. Use words from the box. Write another verse.**

# When I Grow Up

When I grow up, when I grow up,

    I want to _____.

I want to be a _____, just like my mum.

When I grow up, when I grow up,

    I want to _____.

I want to be a _____, just like my dad.

When I grow up, when I grow up,

    I want to _____.

I want to be a _____, just like my aunt.

◆　　◆　　◆

When I grow up, when I grow up,

    I want to _____.

I want to be a _____, just like my _____.

| |
|---|
| **cook good food** **chef** |
| **fly a plane** **pilot** |
| **work in a school** **teacher** |

# Busy Friends

**11** **Read *Busy Friends*. Draw lines to match.**

1. Lee plays the piano.
2. Khalid plays football.
3. John paints pictures.
4. Magda goes to the cinema.
5. Linda takes photos.
6. Pat has dancing lessons.

**a.** She wants to be a photographer.

**b.** He wants to be an artist.

**c.** She wants to be a dancer.

**d.** He wants to be a musician.

**e.** She wants to be an actor.

**f.** He wants to be a footballer.

**12** **Are you busy after school? Tick the boxes to show what you do. Write two sentences.**

1. _____

2. _____

# Review

**13** **Look. Tick *yes* or *no*. Write.**

1. He's an actor.

☐ Yes, he is.   ☑ No, he's a _doctor_____.

2. She's a teacher.

☐ Yes, she is.   ☐ No, she's a _____.

3. She's a dancer.

☐ Yes, she is.   ☐ No, she's a _____.

4. He's a firefighter.

☐ Yes, he is.   ☐ No, he's a _____.

5. She's a scientist.

☐ Yes, she is.   ☐ No, she's a _____.

6. He's a factory worker.

☐ Yes, he is.   ☐ No, he's a _____.

# Cut-out Activity ✂ - - - - - - - - - - - - - -

**A. Cut out.**
**B. Work with a partner. Match. Talk about people and their jobs.**

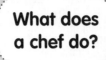

What does a chef do?

A chef cooks food.

| A CHEF | cooks food |
| A TEACHER | dances in a theatre |
| A FACTORY WORKER | does experiments |
| A SHOPKEEPER | flies planes |
| A FIREFIGHTER | helps people get well |
| A DOCTOR | acts in films |
| A MUSICIAN | makes music |
| A SCIENTIST | makes toys |
| AN ACTOR | plays football |
| A DANCER | puts out fires |
| A FOOTBALLER | works in a school |
| A PILOT | works in a shop |

# 6 Every Day

TRACK 18

**1** **Listen and write. Use words from the box.**

| eight | nine | one | six |
|-------|------|-----|-----|

## From Morning to Night

Tick tock, it's _____ o'clock,

_____ o'clock in the morning.

_____ o'clock is time for school.

Hear the bell? That's my warning!

Now it's _____ o'clock, time for lunch,

_____ in the afternoon.

I know that it's lunchtime when I hear this tune.

It's _____ o'clock, homework time,

_____ o'clock in the evening.

Now I get my homework done.

I really like my reading.

Tick tock, it's _____ o'clock.

It's _____ o'clock at night –

time to go to bed, time to turn out the light.

From the morning to the afternoon,

in the evening and at night,

I do all the things I do when the time is right.

**2** **Look and write. Use number words.**

1. It's _____ o'clock.

2. It's _____ o'clock.

3. It's _____ o'clock.

4. It's _____ o'clock.

5. It's _____ o'clock.

6. It's _____ o'clock.

7. It's _____ o'clock.

8. It's _____ o'clock.

9. It's _____ o'clock.

**When** do you do your homework?     I do my homework **in the afternoon**.
**What** do you do after dinner?       I **watch television**.

 **Write *When* or *What*.**

1. _____ does he get dressed?
   He gets dressed in the morning.

2. _____ do they do after school?
   They play football after school.

3. _____ does he have dinner?
   He has dinner in the evening.

4. _____ does she do after dinner?
   She does her homework after dinner.

5. _____ does he do at night?
   He goes to bed at night.

 **Write. Use words from the box.**

| nine o'clock | one o'clock |
| seven o'clock | three o'clock |

1. I get dressed at _____ in the morning.

2. He goes to bed at _____ at night.

3. They have lunch at _____ in the afternoon.

4. They walk home from school at _____ in the afternoon.

**5** **Look. Answer the questions.**

1. What does Mario do in the morning?

   _____

2. What does Mario do in the afternoon?

   _____

3. What does Mario do at night?

   _____

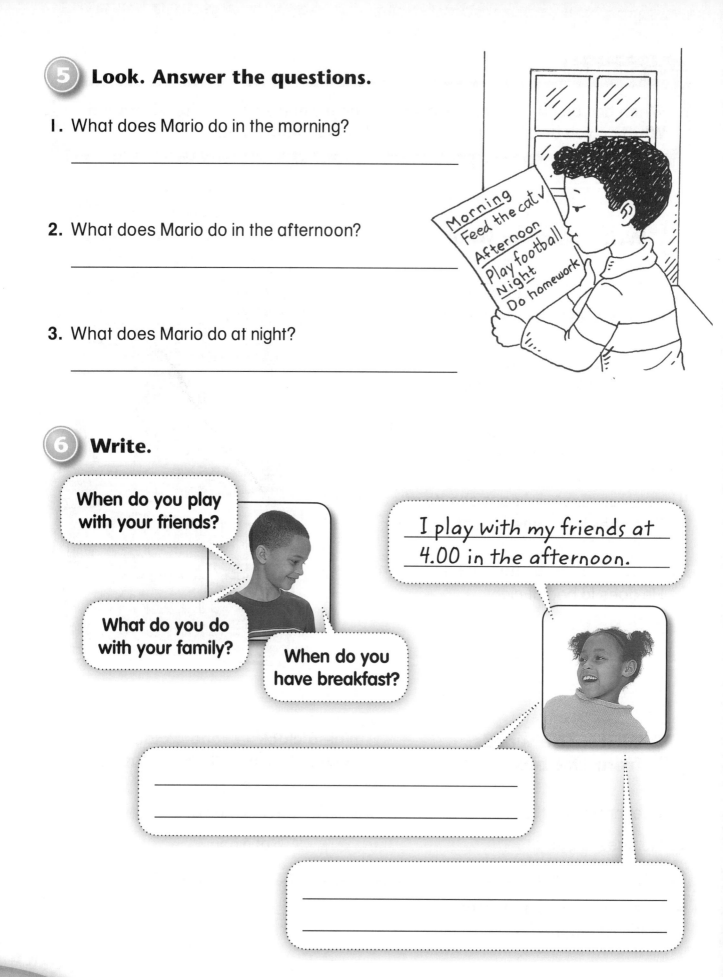

Morning
Feed the cat ✓
Afternoon
Play football
Night
Do homework

**6** **Write.**

When do you play
with your friends?

I play with my friends at
4.00 in the afternoon.

What do you do
with your family?

When do you
have breakfast?

_____

_____

_____

_____

**7** **Circle the best words in the boxes.**

I | wake up
go to bed | in the morning

when the | moon
sun | shines so bright,

I | ride my bike
have breakfast | in the afternoon,

then I | go to school
go to bed | at night!

**8** **What do you do in the afternoon? Write.**
**Draw and colour.**

I _____ in the afternoon.

**9** **Listen and match. Draw lines.**

1. Dan feeds his cat                              a. in the afternoon.

2. They're going to the park          b. at 8.00.

3. They go to bed                              c. every day.

4. Lucy does her homework            d. at 4.00.

5. She and her friends ride their bikes      e. in the morning.

**10** **Listen. Write.**

# Hurry, Hurry!

Oh, no! It's really late!

Wash your  _____ and get your  _____!

Hurry, hurry! Time for school!

Oh, no! It's really late!

Eat your  _____ and brush your  _____!

Hurry, hurry! Time for school!

Oh, no! It's really late!

Get your  _____ and get your  _____!

Hurry, hurry! Time for school!

No, Mum. It isn't late!

Look at the  _____ on the wall!

It's Sunday – no school at all!

# Perfect Penny

**11**   **Read *Perfect Penny*. Tick the boxes.**

1. At 7.00, Penny _____.

   ☐ brushes her teeth

   ☐ has her breakfast

   ☐ feeds her cat

2. At 7.15, Penny _____.

   ☐ gets dressed

   ☐ goes to school

   ☐ has a bath

3. At 7.30, Penny _____.

   ☐ wakes up

   ☐ does her homework

   ☐ gets dressed

4. At 7.45, Penny _____.

   ☐ is ready to leave the bathroom

   ☐ goes to bed

   ☐ has a bath

**12**   **What happens next? What do you think Penny does at 8.00? Write.**

_____

_____

**13**   **What is Penny's favourite colour? How do you know? Write.**

_____

_____

# Review

**14** Look at the clocks. Write the time. Use words from the box.

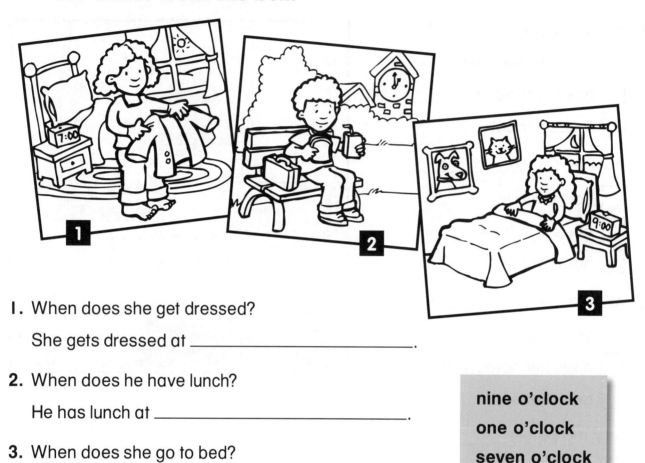

1. When does she get dressed?

   She gets dressed at _____.

2. When does he have lunch?

   He has lunch at _____.

3. When does she go to bed?

   She goes to bed at _____.

> nine o'clock
>
> one o'clock
>
> seven o'clock

**15** Answer the questions.

1. What do you do in the morning?

   _____

2. What do you do at school?

   _____

3. What do you do in the afternoon?

   _____

# Cut-out Activity ✂----------------------

When do you
have breakfast?

I have breakfast
at seven o'clock
in the morning.

**A. Cut and glue.**
**B. Work with a partner. Ask and answer.**

| In the morning | |
|---|---|
| at seven o'clock | |
| at eight o'clock | |
| at nine o'clock | |
| **In the afternoon** | |
| at one o'clock | |
| at four o'clock | |
| **In the evening** | |
| at six o'clock | |
| at seven o'clock | |
| at nine o'clock | |

| | | |
|---|---|---|
| do homework | have breakfast | have dinner |
| have lunch | get dressed | get up |
| go to bed | go to school | play with friends |
| ride a bike | have a bath | watch television |

# Favourite Foods

**1** **Listen and write. Use words from the box. Trace and colour.**

| dessert | fruit juice |
|---------|-------------|
| meat | vegetables |

## Yum, Yum!

Yum, yum!

I like orange juice and apple juice.
I like _____. How about you?
I like carrots and tomatoes.
I like _____.
I like chicken and burgers.
I like all kinds of _____.

Yum, yum! Yum, yum!

I like ice cream and chocolate cake.
I like _____.
I like all kinds of different food.
I like eating.

Yum, yum! Yum, yum!
Yum, yum! Yum, yum!

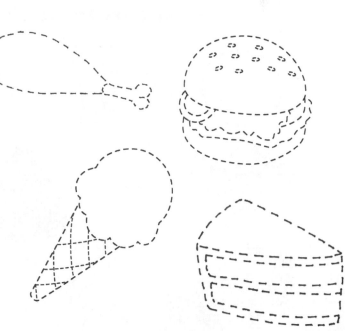

**Write. Use words from the box.**

1. I've got _____ apple.

2. Anna has got _____ cake.

3. Joe has got _____ carrot.

4. Magda has got _____ chicken.

5. Carmen has got _____ burger.

6. Ted has got _____ ice cream.

7. Karen has got _____ tomato.

8. Lee has got _____ orange.

| a |
|---|
| an |
| some |

**3  Look. Draw lines to match.**

| Do | | you | **like** meat? | Yes, | | I | **do**. | | I | | **like** steak. |
| --- | --- | --- | --- | --- | --- | --- | --- | --- | --- | --- | --- |

Do     you  **like** meat?   Yes,   I   **do**.        I     **like** steak.
                               No,    I   **don't**.     I     **don't like** meat.

**Does** | he / she | **like** meat?   Yes, | he / she | **does**.   | He / She | **likes** steak.

No, | he / she | **doesn't**.   | He / She | **doesn't like** meat.

### 4 Look at the chart. Write.

**Does Mary like it?**

| Yes | No |
| --- | --- |

1. Does Mary like chicken?
   _Yes, she does._

2. Does she like strawberries?
   _____

3. Does she like tortilla chips and salsa?
   _____

4. Does she like green beans?
   _____

5. Does Mary like fish?
   _____

6. Does she like burgers?
   _____

7. Does she like cheese and biscuits?
   _____

8. Does she like mangoes?
   _____

### 5 What foods do you like?

_____

_____

_____

**Look. Write *like, likes, don't like* or *doesn't like*.**

1. Julia _____ doesn't like _____ biscuits.

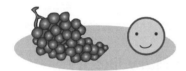

2. I _____ grapes.

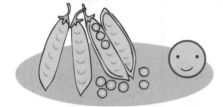

3. John _____ peas.

4. I _____ pineapple.

5. Ricky _____ peppers.

6. I _____ chocolate cake.

7. Hilda _____ cheese.

**7** **Complete the questions.**

Yes, I do.

1. _____
   _____ chicken?

2. _____
   _____ shellfish?

No, she doesn't.

3. _____
   _____ cabbage?

No, I don't.

**8** **What's in the shopping trolley? Find six words.
Circle them.**

```
c a r r o t s p
r m b u q h l y
b i s c u i t s
e l z y k o p f
r k n u l z i i
z o r a n g e s
e g v x w o h h
```

**TRACK 22**

## 9 Listen. Tick *true* or *false*.

|   | | true | false |
|---|---|---|---|
| 1. | The restaurant has got chicken and potatoes. | ☐ | ☐ |
| 2. | She doesn't like chocolate ice cream. | ☐ | ☐ |
| 3. | He wants to drink some orange juice. | ☐ | ☐ |
| 4. | She likes cabbage. | ☐ | ☐ |
| 5. | They want cereal with milk for breakfast. | ☐ | ☐ |

**TRACK 23**

## 10 Listen and write. Use words from the box.

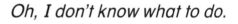

| bread | cereal | cheese | eggs | meats | muffins |
|---|---|---|---|---|---|

# Bobby's Big Breakfast

Here we are at the breakfast buffet.
Come on, Bobby, don't take all day!

*Oh, I don't know what to do.*

*I want steak and _____ and _____, too!*

We're waiting and waiting at the breakfast buffet.
Come on, Bobby, don't take all day!

*Oh, I don't know what to do.*

*I want _____ and jam and _____, too!*

We're waiting and waiting at the breakfast buffet.
Come on, Bobby, don't take all day!

*Oh, I don't know what to do.*

*I want fruit and _____ and cold _____, too!*

# Food Comes from Everywhere

**11** **Read *Food Comes from Everywhere*.**
**Tick *yes* or *no*.**

                                        yes    no

1. Bread comes from wheat.              ☐      ☐

2. Mussels come from trees.             ☐      ☐

3. Cheese comes from cows.              ☐      ☐

4. Fish come from seas and rivers.      ☐      ☐

5. Pine nuts come from chickens.        ☐      ☐

6. Lemons come from trees.              ☐      ☐

7. Pasta comes from cows.              ☐      ☐

8. Eggs come from chickens.            ☐      ☐

**12** **What is your favourite food?**
**Where does it come from? Write.**

*My favourite food is pasta.*
*Pasta comes from wheat.*

My favourite food is _____.

_____ comes from _____.

# Review

13 **Colour the foods. Point and say. Draw lines to match.**

apple

banana

cake

cheese

chicken

lemonade

peas

pie

shellfish

tomato

14 **Answer the questions.**

1. Do you like cabbage? _____, _____.

2. Do you like ice cream? _____, _____.

3. Do you like nuts? _____, _____.

4. Do you like onions? _____, _____.

5. What do you want to eat and drink? _____.

# Cut-out Activity ✂----------------------

A. Cut and glue. Write a tick (✔) or a cross (✗) for foods you *like* or *don't like.*

B. Work with a partner. Talk about what you like and don't like.

Do you like salmon?

No, I don't.

**Foods from animals**

**Foods from plants and trees**

**Foods from water**

| apples ☐ | bananas ☐ | bread ☐ | eggs ☐ | green beans ☐ |
| burgers ☐ | ice cream ☐ | lemons ☐ | mangoes ☐ | pine nuts ☐ |
| popcorn ☐ | shellfish ☐ | steak ☐ | tortilla chips ☐ | trout ☐ |

# Fun at the Zoo

**1** **Listen. Write numbers and words.**

## At the Zoo

*What do you want to see today*
*when we go to the zoo?*
I want to see the (1), (2) and (3)!

_____

*What do you want to see today*
*when we go to the zoo?*
I want to see the (4), (5) and (6), too!

(1) elephants

*What do you want to see today*
*when we go to the zoo?*
Animals from around the world
  that say more than moo!
Let's go to the zoo!

_____

I want to see (7) and (8)
  and (9) and monkeys
  and cheetahs and hippos,
  snakes and polar bears, too.
When we go to the zoo…
Let's go to the zoo!

_____

_____

_____

_____

**2** **Write. Use words from the box.**

| feathers | mouth | neck | tail | teeth |
|---|---|---|---|---|

**1.** A hippo is short.

Its _____ is big.

**2.** A polar bear is big.

Its _____ is short.

**3.** A giraffe is tall.

Its _____ is long.

**4.** A lion is strong.

Its _____ are sharp.

**5.** Peacocks are small.

Their _____ are soft.

| Can a monkey climb a tree? | Yes, it **can**. | |
| Can a monkey catch seals? | No, it **can't**. | can't = cannot |
| Can crocodiles swim fast? | Yes, they **can**. | |
| Can crocodiles climb trees? | No, they **can't**. | |

 **Circle *can* or *can't*.**

1. Giraffes    **can**    **can't**    eat the leaves from tall trees.

2. Cheetahs    **can**    **can't**    run very fast.

3. Snakes    **can**    **can't**    jump high.

4. Monkeys    **can**    **can't**    swing from trees.

5. Elephants    **can**    **can't**    lift heavy things.

**Write *can* or *can't*.**

1. A crocodile _____ climb a tree.

2. A kangaroo _____ jump high.

3. An elephant _____ swim fast.

4. A polar bear _____ catch fish.

5. A lion _____ eat with its sharp teeth.

**5** **Write.**

Can an elephant lift things with its trunk?

Yes, it can.

Can giraffes swing from trees?

_____
_____

_____
_____
_____

_____
_____

**6** **Read and look. Write numbers.**

1. This animal hasn't got legs. It can catch and squeeze animals.

2. This animal has got a short tail and sharp claws. It can catch seals.

3. This animal has got strong legs. It can run very fast.

## Grammar

| | | |
|---|---|---|
| **Has** a hippo **got** a big mouth?<br>**Has** a hippo **got** a long tail? | Yes, it **has**.<br>No, it **hasn't**. | hasn't = has not |
| **Have** lions **got** sharp teeth?<br>**Have** lions **got** long necks? | Yes, they **have**.<br>No, they **haven't**. | haven't = have not |

 **Answer the questions.**

1. Has a giraffe got a long neck?

   _____

2. Has an elephant got feathers?

   _____

3. Have crocodiles got short legs?

   _____

4. Have peacocks got long trunks?

   _____

 **Draw an animal. Talk about your animal. What has your animal got? What hasn't it got?**

**9** **Listen and circle.**

1. a peacock     a hippo     a monkey

2. a polar bear     a cheetah     a kangaroo

3. a snake     a giraffe     an elephant

4. a crocodile     a bird     a snake

5. a dog     a peacock     a cheetah

6. a rabbit     a monkey     a crocodile

**10** **Listen and write. Choose words from the boxes. Write each word two times.**

# Act Like the Animals

1. I can _____ a tree like a monkey,
   and act like a monkey, too.

   I can _____ a tree like a monkey.
   It's your turn – what about you?

2. I can _____ very fast like a cheetah,
   and act like a cheetah, too.

   I can _____ very fast like a cheetah.
   It's your turn – what about you?

3. I can _____ in the water like a crocodile,
   and act like a crocodile, too.

   I can _____ in the water like a crocodile.
   It's your turn – what about you?

climb

run

squeeze

fly

swim

jump

# The Lion and the Rabbit

**11** **Read *The Lion and the Rabbit*. Tick *yes* or *no*.**

|  | yes | no |
|---|---|---|
| 1. King Lion catches Rabbit for his dinner. | ☐ | ☐ |
| 2. King Lion takes Rabbit to a deep well. | ☐ | ☐ |
| 3. King Lion looks at his reflection in the well. | ☐ | ☐ |
| 4. King Lion says, "I am king of this well." | ☐ | ☐ |
| 5. Rabbit jumps into the well because he is happy. | ☐ | ☐ |

**12** **What comes next? Tick one box. Draw.**

☐ Rabbit eats a carrot.

☐ Rabbit sees a crocodile.

☐ Rabbit jumps high.

☐ Rabbit goes home to rest.

# Review

 **13** **Write. Use words from the boxes.
Draw lines to the animals.**

1. An elephant can _____.

2. A polar bear can _____.

3. A kangaroo can _____.

4. A giraffe can _____.

5. A giraffe has got _____.

6. A cheetah has got _____.

7. A monkey has got _____.

8. A kangaroo has got _____.

# Cut-out Activity

**A.** Work with a partner. Cut and glue.

**B.** Talk about what animals can and can't do.

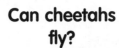

| Animals | can | can't |
|---|---|---|
| monkeys | | |
| crocodiles | | |
| elephants | | |
| giraffes | | |
| kangaroos | | |
| cheetahs | | fly |
| polar bears | | |
| snakes | | |

| | | |
|---|---|---|
| catch food with claws | climb | eat leaves of tall trees |
| fly | jump | jump high |
| lift heavy things | lift things | run fast |
| run very fast | spread their feathers | squeeze animals |
| swim | swim fast | swing from trees |

 # Twelve Months Make a Year

**1 Listen and write.**

## Twelve Months

Thirty days in September,

_____, June and November –

Shorter than the rest I hear,

but _____ months make a year.

Other months have got 31 days.

January, _____ and May,

July, August, _____, December.

Twelve months make a year.

February's got 28 – that's great!

Sometimes _____ –

that's fine.

There's one thing that is

always clear.

Twelve months make a year.

Can I help you to remember

from January to December?

One thing never changes here.

Twelve months make a year.

> How many months
> are there?

| January | February | March | April |
| June | July | August |
| September | October | November | December |

**2** **Look and read. Write *always* or *never*.**

Spain in August

Poland in February

Brazil in January

1. In Poland, he _____ goes swimming in February.

2. In Brazil, I _____ go swimming in January.

3. In Spain, she _____ plays in the snow in August.

4. In Poland, I _____ wear a warm jacket in February.

5. In Brazil, they _____ go skiing in January.

6. In Spain, I _____ wear shorts in August.

7. In my country, I _____ finish school in June.

8. In my country, I _____ have picnics in April.

What do you do in May?     We **always** plant trees in May.
We **never** go on holiday in May.

 **Write about you.**

1. What do you do in December? I always
_____ in December.

2. What do you do in July? I never _____ in July.

3. What do you do in August? I always _____
in August.

4. What do you do in September? I always _____
in September.

Grammar

When **do** | you
they | **go** swimming?     When **does** | he
she | **go** swimming?

 **Write a question.**

1.  _When do they play in the snow?_____
They play in the snow in February.

2. _____
He plants flowers in April.

3. _____
They start school in February.

4. _____
She has a birthday party in March.

5. _____
They go swimming in January.

**5** **Write about you.**

1. What do you do in April?

   I _____ in April.

2. What do you do in December?

   I _____ in December.

3. When do you start school?

   I start school in _____.

4. When do you go swimming?

   I go swimming in _____.

**6** **Look and read. Answer the questions.**

1. What does he do?

   *He plays in the snow.*

   When does he do it?

   _____

2. What do they do?

   _____

   When do they do it?

   _____

3. What do they do?

   _____

   When do they do it?

   _____

Poland in February

Brazil in January

Argentina in February

84

**7** **What month is it? Read and write.**

1. It's between July and September. In some places, it is hot and people go swimming.

   _It's August_ _____

2. It comes right after January. Children in Argentina start school.

   _____

3. It's the month before July. People in Finland celebrate the longest day of the year.

   _____

4. It's between December and February. In many places, it is cold and snows a lot.

   _____

 **8** **What is your favourite month? Why? Write. Draw.**

_____

_____

**9** **Listen and write.**

1. His sister's birthday is in _____.

2  They always have a party in _____.

3. They don't go to the beach in _____.

4. His favourite month is _____.

5. This year, he is going on holiday in _____.

 **10** **Listen. Draw lines to match.**

# Favourite Months

My favourite month is _____.
Do you want to know why?

I always plant flowers and walk in the rain.
My umbrella keeps me dry.

My favourite month is _____.
Do you want to know why?

I always pick apples and jump in the leaves,
and eat plenty of apple pie!

My favourite month is _____.
Do you want to know why?

I always play football and swim in the lake,
and fly my kite in the sky.

 **11** **Write another verse.**

My favourite month is _____. Do you want to know why?

I _____,

and _____.

# My Favourite Month

 **Read _My Favourite Month_. Draw lines to match.**

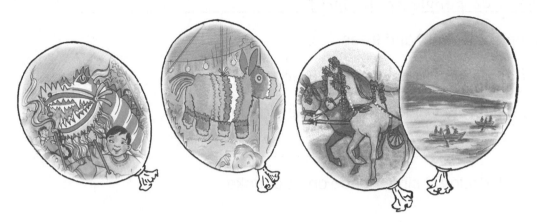

1. People enjoy doing this on this special holiday in Finland.

2. Everyone enjoys watching these on this holiday in China.

3. Children play games like this on this holiday in Mexico.

4. There is a big parade with these on this holiday in Spain.

 **Read. Circle.**

1. What holiday in the story do you like?

| Juhannus | Las Posadas | Feria de Abril | Chinese New Year |

2. What do people like about this holiday?

   **a.** the big fair     **b.** the dragon dances     **c.** boating on the lake     **d.** the nine days of fun

3. This holiday is after May and before October. What is it?

| Las Posadas | Feria de Abril | Juhannus | Chinese New Year |

# Review

**14** **Write questions with *what* or *when*.**

1. _What do people do in April?_

They plant flowers and trees.

2. _When do people celebrate Chinese New Year?_

They celebrate Chinese New Year in January.

3. _____

On my birthday, I sing, dance and eat cake.

4. _____

My birthday is in October.

5. _____

They celebrate the longest day of the year in June.

6. _____

In April, we have a big parade with horses.

7. _____

Some people play in the snow.

8. _____

I start school in September.


**15** **Write *always* or *never*.**

1. Children _____ watch the dragon dance at Chinese New Year.

2. In Poland, we _____ celebrate harvest festival in September.

3. In Finland, we _____ celebrate Juhannus in December.

4. In Argentina, school _____ starts in February.

# Cut-out Activity   &#9986;- - - - - - - - - - - - - -

**A. Cut and glue. Write.**
**B. Work with a partner.**
    **Talk about what you**
    **always do and never do.**

*What do you do in January?*

*I always wear a warm jacket. I never wear shorts.*

| Months of the Year | Always | Never |
|---|---|---|
| January | | |
| February | | |
| March | | |
| April | | |
| May | | |
| June | | |
| July | | |
| August | | |
| September | | |
| October | | |
| November | | |
| December | | |

| | | | |
|---|---|---|---|
| celebrate my birthday | fly a kite | give presents | go on holiday |
| go skiing | go swimming | have a party | have a picnic |
| jump in leaves | pick apples | plant flowers | play football |
| start school | wear a costume | wear a warm jacket | wear shorts |

1. **Say the words. How many times do you hear *t* as in *table*?**

   cat   doctor   elephant   goat   taxi   toes   toy   turtle

2. **Find ten pictures of words with *t* as in *table*. Colour the pictures.**

3. **Look at activity 2. Write ten words with *t* as in *table*.**

   _____robot_____     _____

   _____     _____

   _____     _____

   _____     _____

   _____     _____

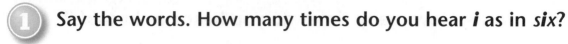

# Sound and Spelling Handbook   *i* as in *six*

**1** Say the words. How many times do you hear *i* as in *six*?

big    fish    gift    kick    kitchen    milk    picnic    sing

**2** Look at the pictures. Write the words with *i* as in *six* in box 1.
Write the words that have not got *i* as in *six* in box 2.

bike            biscuit         fire engine      fish        kitchen
lion            living room     pink             rice        scissors

| fish | lion |
|---|---|
| **1** | **2** |

**1** Say the words. How many times do you hear the same sound as the **c** as in *cat*?

cake    car    catch    cold    biscuit    cow    doctor    picnic

**2** Look at the picture and complete the sentence. Say the sentence.

1. The _____ is walking.

2. That _____ is for the party.

3. The _____ is eating fish.

4. That _____ is new.

5. My uncle is a _____.

6. I like _____.

7. I want that big _____.

8. I want the blue _____.

**1**   **Say the words. How many times do you hear *d* as in *dog*?**

bedroom    dentist    desk    doctor    doll    duck    Friday    red

**2**   **Buddy the dog wants to find his bone. Find the path using words with *d* as in *dog*.**

**Start**

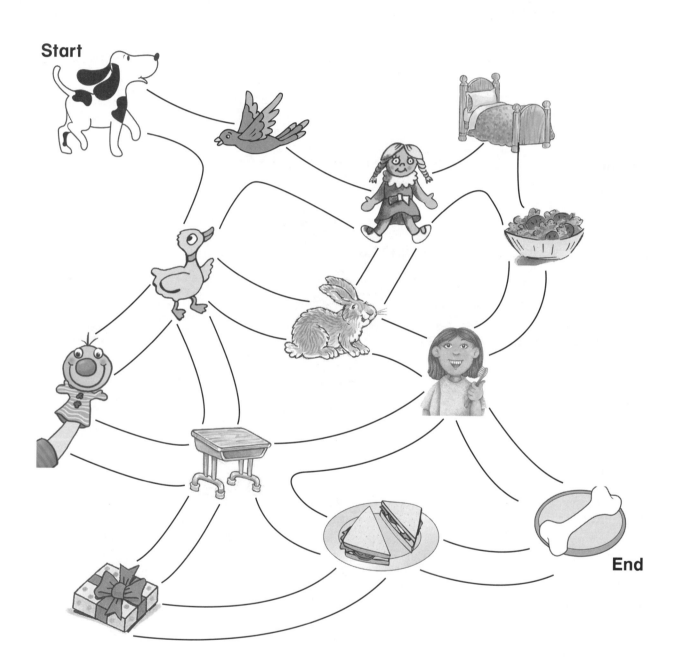

**End**

**1** **Say the words. How many times do you hear *l* as in *lion*?**

school   elephant   family   leg   lemon   little   living room   long

**2** **Draw an X over the picture that hasn't got the same sound as the *l* as in *lion*.**

I.

2.

3.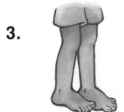

4.

**3** **Look at activity 2. Write the words with *l* as in *lion*.**

_____ _____ _____ _____

_____ _____ _____ _____

**1** **Say the words. How many times do you hear *f* as in *foot*?**

family    farmer    feet    firefighter    five    fly    four    giraffe

**2** **Do the crossword puzzle. Write the words.**

**Down ↓**

1.

2.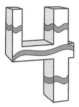

3.

4.

5.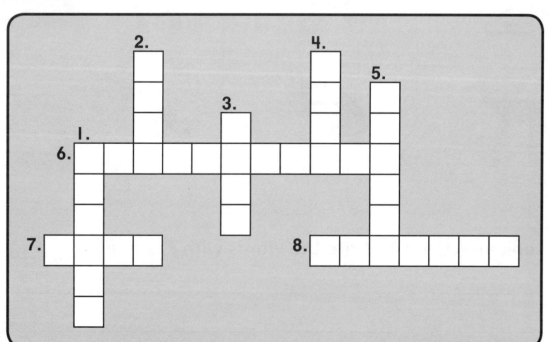

**Across →**

6.

7.

8.

**1** Say the words. How many times do you hear **m** as in **milk**?

arm    bedroom    family    game    jump    marker    milk    monkey

**2** Do the crossword puzzle. Write the words.

**Down ↓**

1.

2.

3.

4.

5.

**Across →**

6.

7.

8.

9.

10.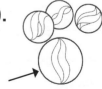

**1** Say the words. How many times do you hear *u* as in *bus*?

cup   duck   fun   hundred   jump   puddle   run   under

**2** Draw an X over the picture that hasn't got the same sound as the *u* as in *bus*.

1.

2.

3.

4.

**3** Look at activity 2. Write the words that have got the same sound as the *u* in *bus*.

_____ _____ _____ _____

_____ _____ _____ _____

# Sound and Spelling Handbook

**h as in *hat***

**①** **Say the words. How many times do you hear *h* as in *hat*?**

he    head    hello    hit    hot    hot dog    hundred

**②** **Unscramble and write eight words with *h* as in *hat*. Match.**

oshue    suhb    ihar    rehos    opiph    ehad    fhis    nadh    tog hod    durdehn

1. _____

2. _____

3. _____

4. _____

5. _____

6. _____

**100**

7. _____

8. _____

Move your counter. Ask and answer or describe the pictures.

6.

7. Where is your television?

8.

9. What do you like doing?

5.

4. What's in your backpack?

3.

2.

1. What does your family like doing?

**START**

Move your counter. Ask and answer.

START

1. Where can you shop for food?

2.

3.

4. What does a pilot do?

FINISH

20.

19.

18. When do you feed your pet?

17.

16.

15. What do you want to be?

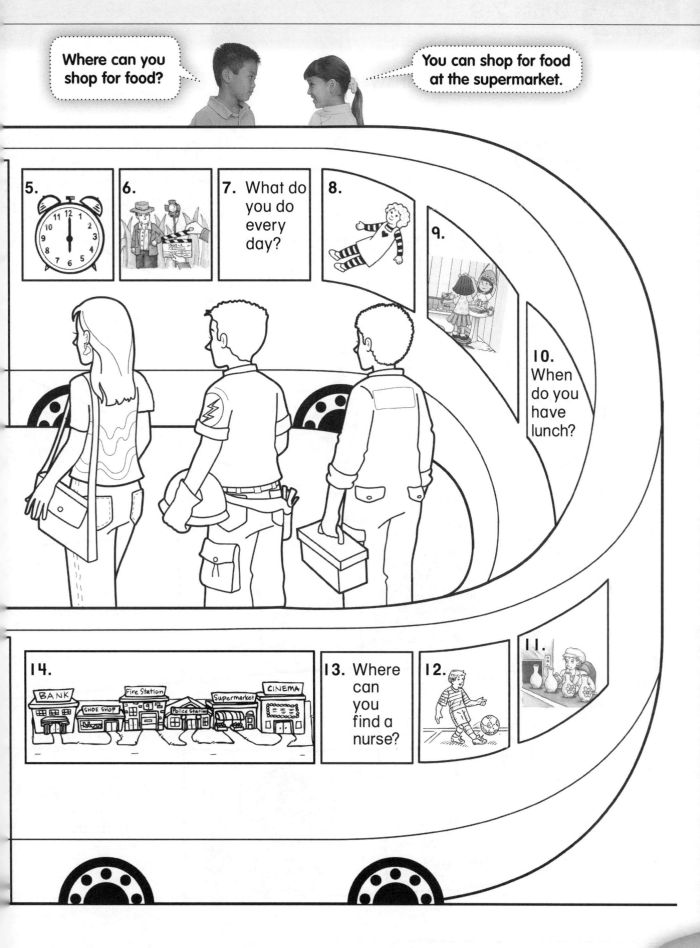

Move your counter. Ask and answer.

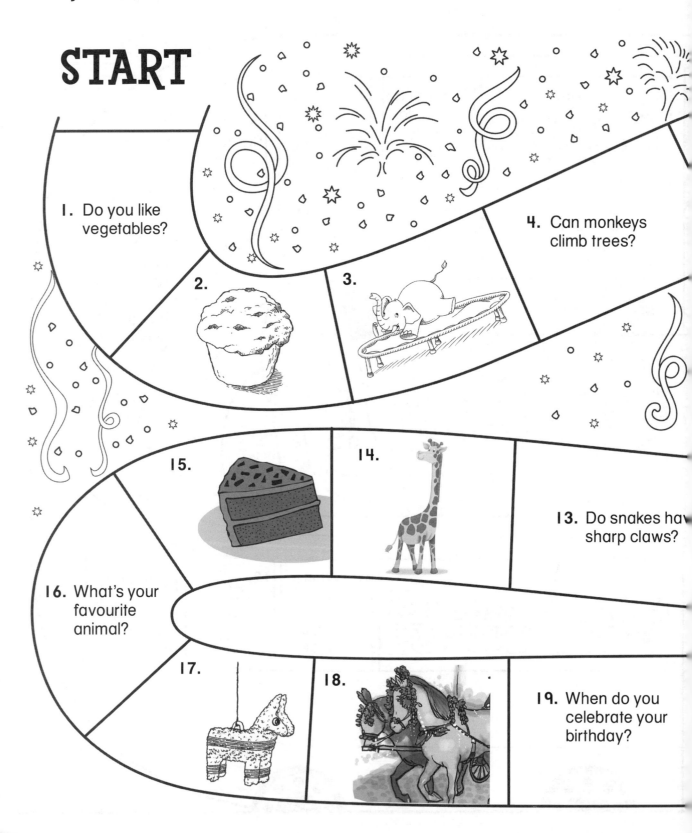

START

1. Do you like vegetables?

2.

3.

4. Can monkeys climb trees?

15.

14.

13. Do snakes have sharp claws?

16. What's your favourite animal?

17.

18.

19. When do you celebrate your birthday?

Review board game, units 7–9

# Grammar and Writing

 **1** **Possessive Adjectives: Complete the sentences.**

| her | his | its | my | our | their | your |

1. Give that notebook to Robert. It's _____ notebook.

2. That present is for Linda. It's _____ present.

3. Jerry and Bill go to school there. It's _____ school.

4. Look at this photo of _____ new baby sister! Now I have two!

5. That cat is thirsty. Put some milk in _____ bowl.

6. We can't watch television. _____ television is broken.

7. Wow! Is that _____ new red bike, Tim?

**2** **Contractions of *Be*: Write.**

1. she is _____          5. I am _____

2. we are _____          6. he is _____

3. it is _____           7. they are _____

4. you are _____

**3** **Simple Present: Circle the correct verb.**

1. Lucy      **get  /  gets**      up at seven o'clock in the morning.

2. Ice cream      **are  /  is**      cold.

3. We      **like  /  likes**      pizza.

4. I      **play  /  plays**      football with my friends.

5. He      **have  /  has**      got a new backpack.

6. They      **have  /  has**      lunch at 1.30.

**Simple Present: Complete the sentences. Use the correct form.**

| brush | climb | draw | skip | like | ride |
|---|---|---|---|---|---|

1. I _____ my teeth after breakfast every day.

2. Our cat _____ the big tree in front of our house.

3. Jenny always _____ pictures of animals.

4. We _____ every afternoon.

5. Mark _____ oranges and bananas.

6. They _____ their bikes to school.

 **Present Continuous: What are they doing? Write sentences.**

1. He _____.
   fly / kite

2. They _____.
   clean / board

3. I _____.
   plant / flowers

4. We _____.
   have / breakfast

## Grammar and Writing

 **Word Order with Adjectives: Unscramble the sentences.**

1. cutting / is / paper / red / she

   _____

2. desk / is / next to / the / brown / window / the

   _____

3. bedroom / is / her / little

   _____

4. is / Frank / a / reading / book / dinosaurs / good / about

   _____

5. Marilyn / busy / today / is

   _____

6. skateboard / is / that / new

   _____

 **Object Pronouns: Write.**

| her | him | it | me | them | you | us | you |

_____    _____    _____    _____

_____    _____    _____    _____